# American Government

# Congress

by Connor Stratton

# www.focusreaders.com

Copyright © 2024 by Focus Readers®, Lake Elmo, MN 55042. All rights reserved. No part of this book may be reproduced or utilized in any form or by any means without written permission from the publisher.

Focus Readers is distributed by North Star Editions:
sales@northstareditions.com | 888-417-0195

Produced for Focus Readers by Red Line Editorial.

Photographs ©: Shutterstock Images, cover, 1, 7, 8, 11, 12, 16; Joyce N. Boghosian/White House, 4; Red Line Editorial, 15; Cameron Smith/White House, 19; Tom Williams/CQ Roll Call/AP Images, 21

**Library of Congress Cataloging-in-Publication Data**
Library of Congress Cataloging-in-Publication Data is available on the Library of Congress website.

## ISBN
978-1-63739-590-5 (hardcover)
978-1-63739-647-6 (paperback)
978-1-63739-760-2 (ebook pdf)
978-1-63739-704-6 (hosted ebook)

Printed in the United States of America
Mankato, MN
082023

# About the Author

Connor Stratton writes and edits nonfiction children's books. He lives in Minnesota.

# Table of Contents

**CHAPTER 1**
## The US Congress 5

**CHAPTER 2**
## The Senate 9

**CHAPTER 3**
## The House of Representatives 13

**CHAPTER 4**
## From Bill to Law 17

**A CLOSER LOOK**
## Overriding a Veto 20

Focus on Congress • 22
Glossary • 23
To Learn More • 24
Index • 24

Chapter 1

# The US Congress

Congress is part of the US **government**. Its main job is passing laws. These laws are rules for the United States. Congress can make new laws. It can change old laws, too.

Congress also has other powers. It chooses if the country goes to war. It is in charge of the country's money, too. Congress plans the country's spending. Congress also plans where that money comes from.

**Did You Know?** Congress meets in the US Capitol. This building is in Washington, DC.

*Chapter 2*

# The Senate

Congress has two parts. These parts are called houses. One house is the Senate. The Senate has 100 members. Each state has two senators.

People in each state choose their senators. They vote in an **election**. The winner becomes a senator. He or she is a senator for six years. Then there is another election. The senator can **run** again.

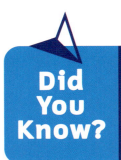

**Did You Know?** Some people serve many years in the Senate.

## Chapter 3

# The House of Representatives

The other part of Congress is the House of Representatives. It has 435 members. Like senators, House members are elected. House members serve for two years. After that, they can run again.

Some states have many House **seats**. Other states have only one. States with more people get more seats. States with fewer people get fewer seats.

**Did You Know?** California has 52 House seats. That is the most of any state.

# House Seats by State

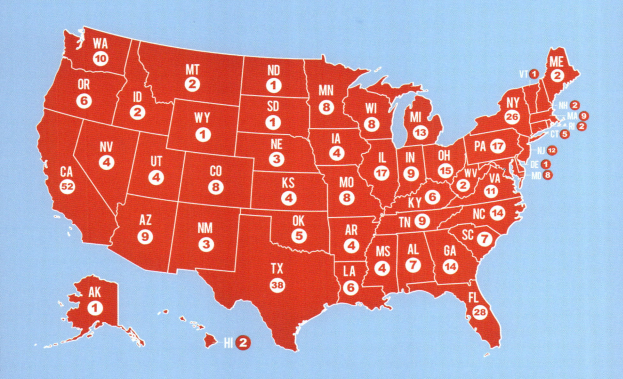

## TITLE I

**SHORT TITLE, ETC.**

**1986 CODE.**—Except... whenever in this title an amer... rms of an amendment to, or ...ion, the reference shall be co... r other provision of the Interna...

### Subtitle A—Individual Tax

### PART I—TAX RATE REFOR

**...ON OF RATES.**

...ction 1 is amended by add... ...ABLE YEARS 201...

### Chapter 4

# From Bill to Law

Members of Congress write **bills**. A bill is a plan for a new law. Other members read the bill. They can argue for or against it.

Next, both houses vote on the bill. A **majority** in each house must vote yes. Only then does the bill pass. After that, the bill goes to the **president**. The president can sign it. Then the bill becomes a law.

**Did You Know?** Congress is one of three parts of the US government. These parts are known as branches.

A Closer Look

# Overriding a Veto

Sometimes the president does not sign a bill. This is called a veto. Often, that bill does not become a law. But Congress can **override** a veto. The Senate and the House vote again. Each house needs a two-thirds majority. If that happens, the bill becomes a law.

# FOCUS ON
# Congress

*Write your answers on a separate piece of paper.*

**1.** Write a few sentences explaining how a bill becomes a law.

**2.** Would you want to visit the US Capitol? Why or why not?

**3.** How many seats does each state have in the Senate?
- **A.** 2
- **B.** 100
- **C.** 435

**4.** What happens if a bill does not get a majority in both houses of Congress?
- **A.** It becomes a law.
- **B.** It does not become a law.
- **C.** It goes to the president to sign.

*Answer key on page 24.*